# Only One of Me

## SELECTED POEMS BY
## James Berry

MACMILLAN CHILDREN'S BOOKS

# For Myra

This collection first published 2004
by Macmillan Children's Books
a division of Macmillan Publishers Limited
20 New Wharf Road, London N1 9RR
Basingstoke and Oxford
www.panmacmillan.com

Associated companies throughout the world

ISBN 0 330 41831 9

A CIP catalogue record for this book is available from the British Library.

Printed by Mackays of Chatham plc, Chatham, Kent.

# Contents

# Isn't My Name Magical?

# Playing a Dazzler

## A Nest Full of Stars

FROM *My Sister's Secret Notebook*

## New Poems

# Introduction

This book is a mixture of all the books of poems I have written for children. It is great to see poems from these different sources brought together in one big selection. I am asking you to have a look and see what catches your eye and perhaps even stirs your feelings.

I will tell you that when I went to my village school in Jamaica, West Indies, in the 1930s, I liked poems. But all the poems we read and studied at school were about life in the United Kingdom. Now changes have happened. I would be very happy to know that poems here work to stir young people's thoughts, feelings, activities and general experiences, in both the Caribbean and the UK particularly. Yet I also hope and believe, that because poems have a way of working in unexpected ways in the imagination, children from anywhere may well relate to poems here and share their varied stories.

Looking a bit into each section, I'll pick out a few of my favourite poems.

In *When I Dance*, I have a great attachment to 'Letter From Your Special Big Puppy Dog'. It always amuses me to think of an owner picking up this enthusiastic over-the-top letter from an affectionate puppy.

Have a look at 'Happenings' in *Isn't My Name Magical?* It seems simple – 'One thing happens/another thing happens . . .' – but this way of noting builds up a picture that might make you laugh.

From *Playing a Dazzler* I'll choose 'Childhood Tracks', a poem that is a series of pictures, sounds, tastes and smells that take me back to the Caribbean.

*A Nest Full of Stars*, my latest book, is full of favourites, but I'll just pick out one popular poem, 'Gobble-Gobble Rap', a joyful celebration of the mouth and of eating. Do read this aloud in real rap fashion.

There are just four poems to give you a little flavour of the book. I leave you to enjoy all the rest.

*James Berry*

# When I Dance

# Seeing Granny

Toothless, she kisses
with fleshy lips
rounded, like mouth
of a bottle, all wet.

She bruises your face
almost, with two
loving tree-root hands.

She makes you sit, fixed.
She then stuffs you
with boiled pudding and lemonade.

She watches you feed
on her food. She milks
you dry of answers
about the goat she gave you.

# Listn Big Brodda Dread, Na!

My sista is younga than me.
My sista outsmart five-foot-three.
My sista is own car repairer
and yu nah catch me doin judo with her.

      I sey I wohn get a complex
      I wohn get a complex
      Then I see the muscles my sista flex.

My sista is tops at disco dance.
My sista is well into self-reliance.
My sista plays guitar and drums
and wahn see her knock back double rums.

      I sey I wohn get a complex
      I wohn get a complex
      Then I see the muscles my sista flex.

My sista doesn mind smears of grease and dirt.
My sista'll reduce yu with sheer muscle hurt.
My sista says no guy goin keep her phone-bound –
with own car mi sista is a wheel-hound.

      I sey I wohn get a complex
      I wohn get a complex
      Then I see the muscles my sista flex.

# Scribbled Notes Picked Up by Owners, and Rewritten
## because of bad grammar, bad spelling, bad writing

## Letter signed – YOUR ONE BABY-PERSON.

I know you like me
because you know I like to be tossed up
in the air and caught
and I know you're best
at making laughs.
You know it's great
when you coo and coo on me in smiles
with hugs and tickles and teases.
I rub my legs together.
I do my baby-dance on my back.
My fist hangs on your thumb.
I chuckle. I chuckle, saying
'This face over me is great!'
I say GA, GA, and you know I say
Go-Ahead, Go-Ahead. Make
funny faces talk, sing,
tickle. Please. Make me chuckle
this time, next time,
every time. Now. Please.

## Letter from YOUR
## SPeCiAl-BiG-pUPPy-DOg.

You know I'm so big
I'll soon become a person.
You know I want to know more
of all that you know. Yet
you leave the house, so, so often.
And not one quarrel between us.
Why don't you come home ten times
a day? Come tell me the way
your boss is bad? See me sit,
Listening, sad? And you know,
and I know, it's best
when you first come in.
You call my name. And O
I go starry-eyed on you,
can't stop wagging, jumping,
holding, licking your face,
saying, 'D'you know – d'you know –
you're quite, quite a dish!'
Come home – come call my name –
every time thirty minutes pass.

## Letter from Your
## KitTeN-cAT-AlMoSt-BiG-CaT.

You tell me to clear up
the strings of wool off
the floor, just to see how
I slink out the door. But O
you're my mum. Fifty times
big to climb on. You stroke
my back from head to tail.
You tickle my furry throat,
letting my claws needle your side,
and my teeth nibble your hand
till I go quiet. I purr.
I purr like a poor boy
snoring, after gift of a dinner.
I leap into your lap only
to start everything over.

# From Your COloURfUl-GUiNea Pig.

You come to me. I shriek
to you, to let you know
I'm a found friend
you can depend on. I know
you long to learn my language.
You talk to me over
and over, in lots
of little words. I listen,
going still, with a quiet heart.
My eyes should go
all in a brighter shine.
Watch my eyes.
Listen to my shriek.
You'll hear what I say.

# Letter from YOuR RaBblT.

To you, who belongs to me.
I listen. You know that.
Come see me. Now.
After. Soon. Later. Again.
All Time – talk
with same words you bring
on my face like daybreak
everyday. Stroke me like wind
passing. Then you've come
for heads to be lost together
in a hole in the ground,
in dreams about fields
grown and overgrown.
Watch my ears, you'll see
I catch all you say.
Feel my eyes on you
and you'll hear
'I have space for you
to huddle, in my bed.'

# Letter from YOUR horse.

Though I'm sort of high up and big
I don't boast. I'm not snooty.
I don't get easily cross.
When you come to me, come
with a long rope of talk
like I'm a soppy dog.
Stroke me with looks, voice,
hands, together saying,
'Hello big fellow!
Handsome big fellow,
you're a joy on the eye
with broad back under sky.
You're swift like flits
of lightning lifts of feet,
but stand still
to listen to human parrot.'
You talk like that,
I nuzzle you.
Hear when I say,
'Come walk with me,
clop-clopping,
with me, side by side.'

**You see, I sign a letter
myself Pig.**

But O most of all
I want you to see
I want us to dig together,
wallow together and share
one bath. I want us to walk
together, all muddy and smart.
I want you to have
my work and my fun.
You give me food, you're gone.
You forget and forget and forget
that if you scratch my back
or rub my belly on and on,
ever so weak I go.
I lie down. I stretch out.
I grunt. I grunt, saying
'Don't. Don't. Don't.
Don't you stop stroking.'

# A Toast for Everybody Who is Growin

Somebody who is growin
is a girl or a boy –
I tell yu is a girl or a boy –
with hips gettn broader
than a lickle skirt
and shoulders gettn bigger
than a lickle shirt,
wantin six teachers
through the misery of maths
and one – only one –
who never ever get cross.
O, the coconut –
it come from so far
yu think it would-a get
hello, from a hazelnut.

Somebody who is growin
is a girl or a boy –
I tell yu is a girl or a boy –
who ride a bus to school
like an empty pocket fool
yet really well wantin
own, own-a, BMW
to cruise up West and North
and all around SW.
O, the pineapple –
it come from so far
yu think it would-a get
hello, from a apple.

Somebody who is growin
is a girl or a boy –
I tell yu is a girl or a boy –
who will never get rich
from a no-inflation boom,
will share no Dallas banquet
that come in own sitting room,
to keep a bodypopper
with a crummy-crummy supper.
O, yu think it would-a mek
a stone scream
rollin down a hill
jumpin in-a stream.
But, in spite of everythin,
everybody who's growin
GO ON, nah! GO ON. Jus do that thing.

# A Different Kind of Sunday

You go to church in England,
it isn't the bright Caribbean day,
isn't orange and mango ripening
with fowls raking about under bush.
It's not a donkey and mule holy day
after they'd bathed in sea in sunrise,
not the same dream of Jesus
when you are melting,
though you fan yourself and everybody else.

You go to church in England,
it's no banana and coconut trees
making a little breeze look merry
in middleday sunhot
when goats pant in mottled shades.

You go to church in England,
cleaned-up people listen to parson
but trucks aren't parked in palmtree yards
when loose boys fix bicycles,
birdsong stripes the day like ribbons,
the sea has a Sabbath day seasound.

You go to church in England,
parson is same preacher-Paul strong-man
beating the air to beat up badness
but John-crows don't glide around blue sky
to be looked at out of window.
And good things at the end aren't
like best lemonade, iced up,
and dinner added-to all week
to go with family jokes kept Sunday-quiet
before the walking-out in evening shadows.

You go to church in England,
you sit in a groan
of traffic on and on around you,
where, O, the sun is so so forgetful.

# Breath Pon Wind

Mi mum is funny, funny, yu know.
Listn to mi mum to mi big brodda, na –

'Boy! Have yuself lost in-a youth gang.
yu only can see notn wrang.

Yu cahn see, cos yu eyes
no longa yu own eyes,
cos they well-well seized in-a gang control
to get all a yu, spoilers, feelin bold,
to get all yu good sense gone too scarce
and it easy to throw brick pon glass place
and yu know notn ow yu come lan
straight in-a police van.

Boy! Yu mus learn to turn man, yes,
but noh by gettn in-a fool-fool mess.
A boy dohn have to go all boasify –
bloated, to mek him good smart guy –
so it easy to toss foot up pon train seat
and smoke cigarette like a stupid sweet.

Boy! Yu goin answer me?
Yu goin answer me?
Yu a-hear what I a-sey
or all is waste breath wind blow away?'

Wahn hear mi mum to mi big brodda, na!
Mi mum is funny, funny, yu know.

*boasify – to be conceited and boastful.*

# Mum Dad and Me

My parents grew among palmtrees,
in sunshine strong and clear.
I grow in weather that's pale,
misty, water or plain cold,
around back streets of London.

Dad swam in warm sea, at my age.
I swim in a roofed pool.
Mum – she still doesn't swim.

Mum went to an open village market
at my age. I go to a covered
arcade one with her now.
Dad works most Saturdays.

At my age Dad played
cricket with friends.
Mum helped her mum, or talked
shouting halfway up the hill.
Now I read or talk on the phone.

With her friends Mum's mum washed
clothes on a river-stone. Now
washing machine washes our clothes.
We save time to eat to TV,
never speaking.
My dad longed for a freedom in Jamaica.
I want a greater freedom.
Mum prays for us, always.

Mum goes to church
some evenings and Sundays.
I go to the library.
Dad goes for his darts at the local.

Mum walked everywhere, at my age.
Dad rode a donkey.
Now I take a bus
or catch the underground train.

# Black Kid in a New Place

I'm here, I see
I make a part of a little planet
here, with some of everybody now.

I stretch myself, I see
I'm like a migrant bird
who will not return from here.

I shake out colourful wings.
I set up a palmtree bluesky
here, where winter mists were.

Using what time tucked in me, I see
my body pops with dance.
Streets break out in carnival.

Rooms echo my voice. I see
I was not a migrant bird. I am
a transplanted sapling, here, blossoming.

# Let Me Rap You My Orbital Map

At a disco girls cluster and dance me in,
at a party everyone knows I don't take gin.
I walk in a room that's tangled with fight
I cool it, calm it, make things right –
shove a head back on where it came adrift;
shove an arm back on where it had left.
Kisses wash me for that ease in my tough;
gifts are piled on me though already I've enough

      Cos – I'm a social rover,
      I overspend – I'm a goldcard lover,
      but man, you know, rhythm's the thing
      and girl, you know, I got the style that sings.

I fix it at cricket I'm top run-getter,
fix it at football I'm that wall-goalkeeper.
My chest is first on the tape when I run;
I box ten rounds – it's ten k.o's of fun.
Yet who can say I do not care –
for a change, I pamper, I fix my hair.
I meet the town, I expose what's vile;
I meet my crowd I'm all a smile.

      Cos – I'm a social rover,
      I overspend – I'm a goldcard lover,
      but man, you know, rhythm's the thing
      and girl, you know, I got the style that sings.

So warm, my handshake sets people on fire.
Such a storm – ceilings come down when I holler.
I don't stand by and cry I won't be a spy;
I don't tell a private or a worldwide lie
Clothes fashion wise
I'm same me – no disguise
relaxin, creatin, plush in my red Porsche
cruising, or just dashin by – woosh!
        Cos – I'm a social rover,
        I overspend – I'm a goldcard lover,
        but man, you know, rhythm's the thing
        and girl, you know, I got the style that sings.

See, I'm me – one who shuns no test;
one of the few who finds the zest
makin music in my talk
doin a dance in my walk.
And people gasp when I take the stage –
struck with my songs, their sweetness, their rage,
sharing my hop from star to star
as I slam on my silver guitar.
        Cos – I'm a social rover,
        I overspend – I'm a goldcard lover,
        but man, you know, rhythm's the thing
        and girl, you know, I got the style that sings.

# Shapes and Actions

Like roundness of the rotating globe
head and wheel and ball make me think and sigh

Like gliding swim of a small or giant fish
drifting moon makes me think and sigh

Like a tramp's hunt in a waiting dustbin
a fox's city-search for food makes me think and sigh

Like a sloth's slow-motion climb
creeping-in sea-tide makes me think and sigh

Like humans and animals everywhere asleep
inner work of winter trees make me think and sigh

Like unknown red wings taking off in flight
flame-leaps in open space make me think and sigh

# A Story about Afiya*

Afiya has fine black skin
that shows off her white clothes
and big brown eyes that laugh
and long limbs that play.
She has a white summer frock
she wears and washes every night
that every day picks on something
to collect, strangely.

Afiya passes sunflowers and finds
the yellow-fringed black faces there,
imprinted on her frock, all over.
Another time she passes red roses
and there the clustered bunches
are, imprinted on her frock.

She walks through high grass and sees
butterflies and all kinds
of slender stalks and petals
patterned on her back and front
and are still there, after
she has washed her dress.

*Afiya – a Swahili name, meaning health, is
pronounced Ah-fee-yah*

Afiya stands. She watches
the sharp pictures in colour,
untouched by her wash.
Yet, next morning, every day,
the dress is cleaned and ready,
hanging white as new paper.

Then pigeons fly up before her
and decorate her dress
with their flight and group design.
Afiya goes to the zoo;
she comes back with two tigers
together, on her back and on her front.

She goes to the seaside;
she comes home with fishes
under ruffled waves
in the whole stretch of sea
imprinted on her dress.

She walks between round and towered
boulders and takes them away,
pictured on her.

Always Afiya is amazed,
just like when she comes home
and finds herself covered
with windswept leaves
of October, falling.

# Leaps of Feeling

There's nothing like a party. Nothing.
　　　Last night
another dream. The swinging roomful
of zodiac signs.
Showplace of trends and flair.
A piece of spectacle – everybody.
Steps unknown rush in and dance you.

　　　Nothing like a party.
Food isn't for table.
Music's a crowd's own age.
Joy of a drink is the slow sweaty sip.
Wit is how it shoots down brilliance.
Malice of a gossip is how
it is spiced up.

　　　Nothing like a party.
A known voice shatters you.
A known hug collects you up.
A new squeeze charges like champagne.
All dream girls. All show blokes.
Dazzlers rave up those who
only manage a glimmer.
To be, you become
a room of pleasure-pulsing.

Nothing like a party. Nothing.
Reality isn't big enough.
Wishes die.
But hopes mount like flames.
Mixes push somebody
here and there over the top.
    It's a night of clusters:
it works leaps of feeling.
Just can't find where else
I'm more discovered.

# When I Dance

When I dance it isn't merely
That music absorbs my shyness,
My laughter settles in my eyes,
My swings of arms convert my frills
As timing tunes my feet with floor
As if I never just looked on.

It is that when I dance
O music expands my hearing
And it wants no mathematics,
It wants no thinking, no speaking,
It only wants all my feeling
In with animation of place.

When I dance it isn't merely
That surprises dictate movements,
Other rhythms move my rhythms,
I uncradle rocking-memory
And skipping, hopping and running
All mix movements I balance in.

It is that when I dance
I'm costumed in a rainbow mood,
I'm okay at any angle,
Outfit of drums crowds madness round,
Talking winds and plucked strings conspire,
Beat after beat warms me like sun.

When I dance it isn't merely
I shift bodyweight balances
As movement amasses my show,
I celebrate each dancer here,
No sleep invades me now at all
And I see how I am tireless.

It is that when I dance
I gather up all my senses
Well into hearing and feeling,
With body's flexible postures
Telling their poetry in movement
And I celebrate all rhythms.

# Quick Ball Man

Bowlerman bowlerman –
O such a wheel-action is quick ball man!

A warrior man
thas such an all-right movement man.

All day him run races,
a-run those poundin riddim paces.

And wicket them a-fly like bullet hit them.
Ball a-hit batsman leg cos it a-fool him.

Batsman a-get caught.
More a-get out fo nought.

More a-come pad-up with runs in them head
but them jus a-come to walk back dead.

And bowlerman is noh jus bowlerman.
The man turn heself now in-a batsman.

And him noh wahn one-one run to get match fix.
Him only wahn six back-a six.

Soh him noh loveless.
Hug-up is regula fram all the mates.

Bowlerman bowlerman –
O such a wheel-action is quick ball man.

# In Play We Play

In play we play
it's stretch we stretch.
Not war we war.
      And I tag along with it.

Get shin clobbered, don't howl.
Get fouled and hurt, don't shout.
Get knee cut, don't bleed.
Get knocked down, don't die.
Stretching game it is.
Not war.
      And I tag along with it.

It's the grunt in our hit-out
they want in our muscles.
Pull of the pack in the race flat out.
Kick in the ball that makes it a goal.
Reach in the arm that nets the ball.
      And I tag along with it.

Run. Jump. Swing. Pull.
Strain!
It's stretch you stretch.
Not war you war.

Whip-up yourself beyond yourself.
Keep pressing till you drop.
It's stretch we stretch.
Win or lose, they tell us,
it's the stretch we want.
       And I tag along with it.

# The Barkday Party

For my dog's birthday party
I dressed like a bear.
My friends came as lions
and tigers and wolves and monkeys.
At first, Runabout couldn't believe
the bear was really me. But
he became his old self again
when I fitted on his magician's top hat.
Runabout became the star, running about
jumping up on chairs and tables
barking at every question asked him.
Then, in their ordinary clothes,
my friend Brian and his dad arrived
with their boxer, Skip. And with us
knowing nothing about it, Brian's dad
mixed the dog's party meat and milk
with wine be brought. We started
singing. Runabout started to yelp.
All the other six dogs joined –
yelping
> *Happy Barkday to you*
> *Happy Barkday to you*
> *Happy Barkday Runabout*
> *Happy Barkday to you!*

# One

Only one of me
and nobody can get a second one
from a photocopy machine.

Nobody has the fingerprints I have.
Nobody can cry my tears, or laugh my laugh
or have my expectancy when I wait.

But anybody can mimic my dance with my dog.
Anybody can howl how I sing out of tune.
And mirrors can show me multiplied
many times, say, dressed up in red
or dressed up in grey.

Nobody can get into my clothes for me
or feel my fall for me, or do my running.
Nobody hears my music for me, either.

I am just this one.
Nobody else makes the words
I shape with sound, when I talk.

But anybody can act how I stutter in a rage.
Anybody can copy echoes I make.
And mirrors can show me multiplied
many times, say, dressed up in green
or dressed up in blue.

Only One of Me

# Boy Alone at Noon

Completely central over me
is this lace of sun
topping trees.

The world is white
and green and shadowy
I am almost enclosed from sky

The river lolls lapping
over rough tongued rocks
and leaf rottings

A dragonfly takes two dips
it flops in again
it goes with a flip

The nutmeg trees
have pods propped with nuts
I smell hot grass

I smell tree blossoms
I wish I could know
a lot of reasons

Busy birds go stateless
I have no government either
My father is strong and pocketless

The track waits to my hut
I better fill my bamboo with water
and go on up

# Coming Home On My Own

I slept with fourteen strange
people, in the youth-hostel room.
All of us had to get up early.
I turned and opened my eyes –
it was bright open daylight.
Right away, everybody turned over
too, woke up, began to talk.
And it was good how we washed,
dressed and made breakfast together.
But we broke up. We separated
on foot, on bicycles
and I by bus – waving goodbye.

# Getting Nowhere

Next week I'll leave school.
Next week, nil, fulltime –
me – for good!

Yonks now
nobody bothered.
No teacher scrawled, 'work harder'.
Or, 'Use your potential'.

They'd twigged on.
Their words were whispers
to a rock. So
They gave up on me.

They had no grasp –
none to give.
Had no power to kick
my motor into clatter.

Not to lift a bat, next week
I'm bowled out for duck.
Year in year out
terrible need took
nothing teachers served.

I couldn't win them.
They couldn't win me.
Their mouthings reached me jammed.
So routines to me will end next week.

Lamp of workshop drawing got built
only as far as the base
and abandoned. Made scrap.

And a relief will grab them.
Relieved, the teachers will sigh –
'Clearly, a non-achiever.'

Next week, I'll leave school
but stay held on poverty street.
Held hostage by myself, they'll say.

# Skateboard Flyer

Please, Mum, please
not again back-to-school
for I-man-skater.
I must rush it, Mum, rush it
and lift up high
over ransacked dustbins
over streets of rubbish
over every tower block
and be highrise – I, up and over.
Mum – enough times you say
you want me off the streets.

Please, Mum, please
not again back-to-school
for free skateboard Rasta.
I must rush it and lift
over bashed-in street lamps
to drop down on moving roller coaster
and lift off over chimney tops
over mashed-up playgrounds –
gliding over, just gliding and gliding.
Mum – enough times you say
you want me off the streets.

Please, Mum, please
not again back-to-school
for I-man-skater
who must rush it
and shoot from star to star
and be gone
over police stations with arrested people
and be gone
over every schooling barrier
and be gone
over the terror of faces.
Please – not school again.
Mum – enough times you say
you want me off the streets.

# It Seems I Test People

My skin sun-mixed like basic earth
my voice having tones of thunder
my laughter working all of me as I laugh
my walk motioning strong swings
it seems I test people

Always awaiting a move
waiting always to recreate my view
my eyes packed with hellos behind them
my arrival bringing departures
it seems I test people

# Dreaming Black Boy

I wish my teacher's eye wouldn't
go past me today. Wish he'd know
it's okay to hug me when I kick
a goal. Wish I myself wouldn't
hold back when an answer comes.
I'm no woodchopper now
like all ancestors.

I wish I could be educated
to the best of tune up, and earn
good money and not sink to lick
boots. I wish I could go on every
crisscross way of the globe
and no persons or powers or
hotel keepers would make it a waste.

I wish life wouldn't spend me out
opposing. Wish same way creation
would have me stand it would have
me stretch, and hold high, my voice
Paul Robeson's, my inside eye
a sun. Nobody wants to say
hello to nasty answers.

I wish torch throwers of night
would burn lights of decent times.
Wish plotters in pyjamas would pray
for themselves. Wish people wouldn't
talk as if I dropped from Mars.

I wish only boys were scared
behind bravados, for I could suffer.
I could suffer a big big lot.
I wish nobody would want to earn
the terrible burden I can suffer.

# What Do We Do with a Variation?

What do we do with a difference?
Do we stand and discuss its oddity
or do we ignore it?

Do we shut our eyes to it
or poke it with a stick?
Do we clobber it to death?

Do we move around it in rage
and enlist the rage of others?
Do we will it to go away?

Do we look at it in awe
or purely in wonderment?
Do we work for it to disappear?

Do we pass it stealthily
or change route away from it?
Do we will it to become like ourselves?

What do we do with a difference?
Do we communicate to it,
let application acknowledge it
for barriers to fall down?

# City Nomad

Indifferent to crowds
indifferent to weather
he goes about arrested.

Schooled on chasms unbridgeable
he uses pain of traps
to communicate

Own jury own court
he waves and gestures
at his own cross-questioning.

Drifting this morning
he arrives and gazes
at the city's river.

It becomes a shore like a dream
where he is lost
and the sea lashes monstrous rocks.

And he's confused
with suggestions of travel –
going and coming and being.

Arms open, legs apart –
a stare and a grin on his face –
he roars and beckons.

He embraces a towering wave, falls
in a shawl of mist and tightens shut eyes
to keep out faces looking down on him.
Drifting again this evening
he searches
for another bed.

One shadowy thought
stays and absorbs
his entire volition –

somehow
somewhere
someone must have wronged him.

# Me go a Granny Yard

Wha mek yu go Granny Yard?
    Me go Granny Yard
    fi go get sorrel drink.
An dat a really really true?
    Cahn yu hear a true?
Yu noh did go fi notn else?
    Dohn yu hear a notn else?

Wha mek yu go Granny Yard?
    Me go Granny Yard
    fi go get bwoil puddn.
An dat a really really true?
    Cahn yu hear a true?
Yu noh did go fi notn else?
    Dohn yu hear a notn else?

Wha mek yu go Granny Yard?
    Me go Granny Yard
    fi go get orange wine.
An dat a really really true?
    Cahn yu hear a true?
Yu noh did go fi notn else?
    Dohn yu hear a notn else?

Wha mek yu go Granny Yard?
　　Me go Granny Yard
　　　fi go get cokenat cake.
　　　　Cahn yu hear a true?
Yu noh did go fi notn else?
　　　Dohn yu hear a notn else?

Wha mek yu go Granny Yard?
　　Me go Granny Yard
　　　fi go get lemonade.
　　　　Cahn yu hear a true?
Yu noh did go fi notn else?
　　　Dohn yu hear a notn else?

Wha mek yu go Granny Yard?
　　Me go Granny Yard
　　　fi go get ginger cookies.
An dat a really really true?
　　　Cahn yu hear a true?
Yu noh did go fi notn else?
　　　Dohn yu hear a notn else?

Wha mek yu go Granny Yard?
　　Me go Granny Yard
　　　fi go hide from punishment.
Fi go hide from punishment?
　　　Fi go hide from punishment!

# Song of the Sea and People

Shell of the conch was sounded,
sounded like foghorn.
Women rushed to doorways,
to fences, to gateways, and watched.
Canoe made from cotton tree
came sailing shoulder high, from up
mountain-pass down to the sea.
> They stared
> at many men under canoe.
> The mothers and children stared.

Shell of the conch was sounded,
sounded like foghorn.
Women rushed to seaside.
Canoes had come in,
come in from way out
of big sea, loaded
with fish, crabs and lobsters.
> They stared
> at sea-catch.
> The mothers and children stared.

Shell of the conch was sounded,
sounded like foghorn.
Women rushed to seaside.
Canoe out of cotton tree had thrown men,
Deep sea swallowed men.
Big sea got boat back.
>    They stared
>    at empty canoe
>    The mothers and children stared.

# Jamaican Song

Little toad little toad mind yourself
mind yourself let me plant my corn
plant my corn to feed my horse
feed my horse to run my race –
the sea is full of more than I know
moon is bright like night time sun
night is dark like all eyes shut
      Mind – mind yu not harmed
      somody know bout yu
      somody know bout yu

Little toad little toad mind yourself
mind yourself let me build my house
build my house to be at home
be at home till I one day vanish –
the sea is full of more than I know
moon is bright like night time sun
night is dark like all eyes shut
      Mind – mind yu not harmed
      somody know bout yu
      somody know bout yu

# Bye Now

Walk good
Walk good
Noh mek macca go juk yu
Or cow go buck yu
Noh mek dog bite yu
Or hungry go ketch yu, yah!

Noh mek sunhot turn yu dry.
Noh mek rain soak yu.
Noh mek tief tief yu
Or stone go buck yu foot, yah!
Walk good
Walk good

# Goodbye Now

Walk well
  Walk well
Don't let thorns run in you
Or let a cow butt you.
Don't let a dog bite you
Or hunger catch you, hear!

Don't let sun's heat turn you dry.
Don't let rain soak you.
Don't let a thief rob you
Or a stone bump your foot, hear!
  Walk well
    Walk well

# Pods Pop and Grin

Strong strong sun, in that look
you have, lands ripen
fruits, trees, people.

Lands love the flame of your gaze.
Lands hide some warmth
of sun-eye for darkness.

All for you pods pop and grin.
Bananas hurry up and grow.
Coconut becomes water and oil.

Palm trees try to fly to you
but just dance everywhere.
Silk leaves of bamboo rustle wild.

And when rain finished falling
winds shake diamonds from branches
that again feel your eye.

Strong strong sun, in you
lands keep ripening
fruits, trees, people.

Birds go on tuning up
and don't care at all –
more blood berries are coming.

Your look strokes up all
summertime. We hear streams running.
You come back every day.

# Hurricane

Under low black clouds
the wind was all
speedy feet, all horns and breath,
all bangs, howls, rattles,
in every hen house,
church hall and school.

Roaring, screaming, returning,
it made forced entry, shoved walls,
made rifts, brought roofs down,
hitting rooms to sticks apart.

It wrung soft banana trees,
broke tough trunks of palms.
It pounded vines of yams,
left fields battered up.

Invisible with such ecstasy –
with no intervention of sun or man –
everywhere kept changing branches.

Zinc sheets are kites.
Leaves are panic swarms.
Fowls are fixed with feathers turned.
Goats, dogs, pigs,
all are people together.

Then growling it slunk away
from muddy, mossy trail and boats
in hedges: and cows, ratbats, trees,
fish, all dead in the road.

# Workings of the Wind

Wind doesn't always topple trees
and shake houses to pieces.

Wind plays
all over woods, with weighty ghosts
all swings in thousands,
swinging from every branch.

Wind doesn't always rattle windows
and push, push at walls.

Wind whistles
down cul-de-sacs and worries
dry leaves and old newspapers to leap
and curl like kite tails.

Wind doesn't always dry out
sweaty shirts and blouses.

Wind scatters
pollen dust of flowers, washes
people's and animals' faces
and combs out birds' feathers.

Wind doesn't always whip up waves
into white horses.

    Wind shakes up
    tree-shadows to dance on rivers,
    to jig about on grass, and hanging
    lantern light to play signalman.

Wind doesn't always run wild
kicking tinny dustbin lids.

    Wind makes
    leafy limbs bow to red roses
    and bob up and down outside windows
    and makes desk papers fly up indoors.

# Light Fabric

Oranges the tree hung around itself
while people were asleep
are miniature suns in their bowl.

Bananas curled in words at the table
are only other spices of land
that came ripe through the door

The apples piled nought-shaped
are other mixes too April made
and September cupped colourfully

# Jamaican Caribbean Proverbs

## On marriage

Befoh yu marry keep two yeye opn, afta yu marry shet
  one.

*Before marriage keep two eyes open, after marriage, shut one.*

## On the way the human condition is similar

Yu neber si kickin-cow widout kickin-calf.

*You never see a cow that kicks who doesn't produce a calf that
  kicks.*

## On how different you can be different from the way you look

Plenty a mauger cow yu si a common, a bull mumma.

*Many an underfed cow in the pasture is mother of a bull.*

## On vanity

Peacock hide him foot when him hear bout him tail.

*The peacock hides its leg when its tail gets praises.*

If nightingale sing too sweet, jealousy wi kill him
  mumma.

*If the nightingale sings too sweetly, jealousy will kill its mother.*

Boastin man brodda a de liard.

*The boaster will make out someone else is the liar.*

## On the need to first protect yourself if you are going to be insulting or abusive

Noh cuss alligator 'long-mout' till yu cross riber.
*Don't call an alligator a 'long-mouth' till you have crossed the river.*

Lickle axe cut down big tree!
*A little axe can cut down a big tree.*

## On being owned as a slave

Cow wha belang a butcher neber sey him bery-well.
*A cow that belongs to a butcher never says 'I'm very well.'*

'Good bwoy' a nickname fi fool.
*'Good boy' is a fool's nickname.*

## On being disadvantaged

Hungry-Belly and Full-Belly noh walk same pass.
*The rich and the poor do not meet.*

Call tiger 'Massa' him still nyam yu.
*Call a tiger 'Master' he'll still eat you.*

## On feeling hardships are unfair

Jackass sey de worl noh leble.
*The donkey says the world isn't level ground.*

Racktone a riber-battam nah know sun-hot.
*A stone at the bottom of the river doesn't know the heat of the sun.*

## On scapegoating

Cos parrot noisy-noisy, dem sey a dem one nyam up
banana.
*Because parrots are chatterers people say they are the only ones
who eat up the fruits.*

## On how when somebody gets bad treatment you too could get the same

De tick wha flog de black dog wi whip de white.
*The same stick that flogs the black dog will also flog the white
one.*

## On relying on your own initiative

Noh wait till drum beat befoh yu grine yu axe.
*Don't wait till you hear the drum beat before you grind your axe.*

Yu cahn stap bud fram a-fly ober yu, but yu can stap him
a-mek nes pon tap a yu head.
*You can't stop a bird from flying over you, but you can stop it from
making a nest on top of your head.*

## On support

If yu back monkey him wi fight tiger.
*If you back a monkey he'll fight a tiger.*

**On the way an angry noise can be a useless threat**
Dog-bark neber frightn moon!
*A dog's bark isn't going to frighten the moon.*

Trouble never blows conch shell when it's coming.

Stump-a-foot* man can't kick with his good foot.

Is a blessing me come me see you: eye-to-eye joy is a love.

Is better to walk for nothing than sit down for so-so.

Good-friend you can't buy.

Stretch your hand and give it's a God own grace.

*\* Stump-a-foot - stumpy or one-legged*

Isn't My Name Magical?

# Happenings

One thing happens
another thing happens.
A cup slips, it falls,
it crashes into pieces.
The cat leaps, she rushes,
she bangs herself through the catdoor.
'CAAAW!' a crow says, sitting
in the treetop at the garden fence

One thing happens
another thing happens.
An apple drops, from its branch.
It rolls, it stops; a dry leaf
holds it, like a saucer.
'SEEE, SEEE, SEEE, SEEE!'
a strange bird screams,
sitting there in the apple tree.

One thing happens
another thing happens.
Wind lifts off a lady's hat.
It flies, it swirls, it dips,
it falls in the park pond.
A small dog leaps into the water, gets the hat
and gives it to the lady.
A big Boxer who watched goes deep-voiced,
'WOW WOW! WOW WOW!'

# Doesn't a Difference Make You Talk?

Kim's dad watches football shouting vengeance
My dad watches cricket in silent endurance

A man on the bus had hair in his ear
His lady beside him had a clean ear

O the cat zipped up into the tree
And the dog managed only two paws up the tree

My dad goes all sandals and shorts in the summer
Kim's dad's all wellingtons and noisy lawn mower

My class teacher is shrieky and fussy
My dance teacher is cuddly but isn't she messy?

# Isn't My Name Magical?

Nobody can see my name on me.
My name is inside
and all over me, unseen
like other people also keep it.
Isn't my name magical?

My name is mine only.
It tells I am individual,
the one special person it shakes
when I'm wanted.

Even if someone else answers
for me, my message hangs in air
haunting others, till it stops
with me, the right name.
Isn't your name and my name magic?

If I'm with hundreds of people
and my name gets called,
my sound switches me on to answer
like it was my human electricity.

My name echoes across playground,
It comes, it demands my attention.
I have to find out who calls,
who wants me for what.
My name gets blurted out in class,
it is terror, at a bad time,
because somebody is cross.

My name gets called in a whisper
I am happy, because
My name may have touched me
with a loving voice.
Isn't your name and my name magic?

# Dreena's Picture that Makes People Laugh

It is in my drawing book.
The picture is really true
how Daddy turned into a barrel
round as a hoop.
Mummy has straight stick arms
and hands cutting flowers.
I am the tallest
and I wear a broad white hat
and a wide red scarf.
My bigger brother is there
just a sad green-faced puppy sitting.
That day, he'd been really nasty to me.

# Sister and Brother

My sister sits
Like fallen feather in a chair
My brother tumbles in from upstairs

My sister speaks
For ears close in the room
My brother shouts through walls and rooms

My brother simply sits
And gets cross with his maths
My sister sails through her maths

My brother cooks
Like a four-star chef
My sister cooks and the food gets left

My sister waits on and on
Like a listening doctor
My brother jabbers through teas and dinners

My sister sings the blues
My brother hurriedly pulls on
His running shoes

# Delroy the Skateboard Roller

I dance and dance myself away from here
as a skateboard flyer,
as a boy space-walker,
as a dancer-boy explorer.

In my deep sea gear
I have my deep sea flair.
I do my underwater walk
surrounded by sharks.

And how I spin and wheel round on my top,
how I body-break and body-pop,
people's legs take off on a hop
thinking they can't stop.

And because it's all a body full of joy –
in the boy Delroy
like a man employed –
I am a dancer-boy explorer
a dancer-boy explorer.

# Occasion

On, on – it's on.
The music stings, the music bites.
The roomful breaks up body shapes.
And everybody is a bobbing head here.
Everybody is a mover everywhere.
Beat mover Danny is a blue-jeaned rocker;
Gill in a Superman-shirt is a reggae pulser.
O, making a hop of it, we are rocking it.
Isn't this all we ever want to do?

Arms come. Arms go. Sounds are hot.
Legs go astray, all crazy, the lot.
Disorderly bodies get in a muddle;
other hips move with a good firm wiggle.
Gary dances in a tiger-head shirt;
Sue does hers in a flared red skirt.
O, rock it! Writhe! Stamp it! Jump!
Isn't this all we ever want to do?

Each one is a scatterbrained music fool,
everyone is mad, but everything's cool.
Two girls dance together, in purple jump-suits;
Barry moves alone in his white sneaker boots.
Mark wants to cling;
Jane breaks it and does her own trotting.
O, music! You are such a twitch maker!
Isn't this all we ever want to do?

   On, on – it's on.
Fat legs and thin legs prance about;
Sonia mouths the music with a curled mouth.
All of us in our carnival colours
just go on like real carnival revellers
with nobody, nobody, wanting to stop
in this on and on with this hot, hot, hop
in having all one say –
'No jump-up is ever better than a friend's
                    HAPPY BIRTHDAY.'

# Playing a Dazzler

# Childhood Tracks

Eating crisp fried fish with plain bread.
Eating sheared ice made into 'snowball'
with syrup in a glass.
Eating young jelly-coconut, mixed
with village-made wet sugar.
Drinking cool water from a calabash gourd
on worked land in the hills.

Smelling a patch of fermenting pineapples
in stillness of hot sunlight.
Smelling mixed whiffs of fish, mango, coffee,
mint, hanging in a market.
Smelling sweaty padding lifted off a donkey's back.

Hearing a nightingale in song
in moonlight and sea-sound.
Hearing dawn-crowing of cocks, in answer
to others around the village.
Hearing the laughter
of barefeet children carrying water.
Hearing a distant braying of a donkey
in a silent hot afternoon.
Hearing palmtrees' leaves rattle
on and on at Christmas time.

Seeing a woman walking in loose floral frock.
Seeing a village workman with bag and machete
under a tree, resting, sweat-washed.
Seeing a tangled land-piece of banana trees
with goats in shades cud-chewing
Seeing a coil of plaited tobacco
like rope, sold, going in bits.
Seeing children playing in schoolyard
between palm and almond trees.
Seeing children toy-making in a yard
while slants of evening sunlight slowly disappear.
Seeing an evening's dusky hour lit up
by dotted lamplight.
Seeing fishing nets repaired between canoes.

# This Carry-on of Two Boys Over Kim

'Kim and me make one;
anybody else makes none.'
  **'Kim and me heat up a room.'**
'Kim knows you aren't dumb cos you don't know better,
you're dumb cos you don't matter.'
  **'Kim knows, your type scatters
  dustbins at old people's doorways.'**
'Leave off that *Kim Kim* from a rotten tongue.'
  **'Kim's eyes are hypnotists.'**
'Kim's voice sets me up a chuckling idiot.'
  **'Kim's warm lips shut me up.'**
'Her round hips turn me on to stutter.'
  **'Her armful of waist turns me on to worship.'**
'Mind I don't scatter your teeth like a smashed cup!'
  **'Mind I don't dislodge your face!'**
'If you don't know, our regular haunts happen twosome.'
  **'If *you* don't know, after our recent fling
  she took my secret engagement ring.'**
'When high tide swept away her bathing costume
I took her home dressed in moonlight.'
  **'*You*, in Kim's plans –
  you pimply face pig, you stink!'**

'*You* are dumbstruck, on the ground; Kim and me fly
upsidedown, two hundred miles an hour, rollercoasting.'
   '*You* **leave Kim alone!**
   **Or get yourself missing, stiff, on the dump site.**'
'You leave Kim alone.
Or risk a left arm with everything right!'
   '**Mind! Mind you don't hide, rotting.**'
'Look! There goes Kim.
Kim – arm-in-arm with Tim!'

# Playing a Dazzler

You bash drums playing a dazzler;
I worry a trumpet swaying with it.

You dance, you make a girl's skirt swirl;
I dance, I dance by myself.

You bowl, I lash air and my wicket;
I bowl, you wallop boundary balls.

Your goal-kick beat me between my knees;
my goal kick flies into a pram-and-baby.

You eat off your whole-pound chocolate cake;
I swell up halfway to get my mate's help.

My bike hurls me into the hedge;
your bike swerves half-circle from trouble.

I jump the wall and get dumped;
you leap over the wall and laugh, satisfied.

I touch the country bridge and walk;
you talk and talk.

You write poems with line-end rhymes;
I write poems with rhymes nowhere or anywhere.

Your computer game screens monsters and gunners;
my game brings on swimmers and courting red birds.

# Thinking Back on Yard Time

We swim in the mooneye.
The girls' brown breasts float.
Sea sways against sandbanks.

We all frogkick water.
Palm trees stand there watching
with limbs dark like our crowd.

We porpoise-dive, we rise,
we dog-shake water from our heads.
Somebody swims on somebody.

We laugh, we dry ourselves.
Sea-rolling makes thunder
around coast walls of cliffs.

Noise at Square is rum-talk
from the sweaty rum bar
without one woman's word.

Skylarking, in our seizure,
in youthful bantering,
we are lost in togetherness.

Our road isn't dark tonight.
Trees – mango, breadfruit – all,
only make own shapely shadow.

Moon lights up pastureland.
Cows, jackass, all, graze quietly.
We are the cackling party.

# Children's Voices

Caves of bats crisscross
under sky of open dusk.
Fowls crouch in with leaves.
Cows call their pent calves.

Flame-tree is quiet, like a hill
carved into a colourful umbrella.
Shouts and laughter clap round
night shaded fruits hanging
and animals grazing.

Children will go on
flinging wide their last
shrieked fun to stars, and delay
that interfering break of sleep.

# Night Comes Too Soon

Here now skyline assembles fire.
The sun collects up to leave.
Its bright following paled,
suddenly all goes. Dusk rushes
in, like door closed on windowless room.
Children go a little sad.

Fowls come in ones and groups
and fly up with a cry
and settle, in warm air branches.
Tethered pigs are lounging
in dugout ground.

Muzzled goat kids make muffled
cries. Cows call calves locked away.
Last donkey-riders come homeward
calling 'Good night!'
Children go a little sad.

Knives-making from flattened
big nails must stop. Kite ribs
of tied sticks must not develop.
Half shapes growing into bats
and balls, into wheels and tops
must cease by night's veto.

And, alone on shelves, in clusters
on the ground in corners, on
underhouse ledges, these
lovable embryos
don't grow in sleeptime.
Children go a little sad.

Bats come out in swarms.
Oil lamps come up glowing
all through a palmtree village.
Everybody'll be indoors
like logs locked up.
Children go a little sad.

Only One of Me

# Absent Player

Ball games her agony
at rounders she was posted out
and placed at the furthest
possible position
under a tree almost.

Lost, as usual, dreaming,
she heard some vague panic noises
breaking through, as if, desperate,
the whole team were shouting
'Catch the ball! Catch the ball! Catch it!'

She slowly turned her face upwards.
She did not see the ball,
but, it aimed at a resistance
and came down straight, smack
onto a well-shaped mouth.

Her front teeth were loosened
in blood. She lay on the grass.
No way could she tell any
sympathy from her boiling rage
around her. She cried, quietly.

# Sharing is an Open Game

Cricket ball runs errands
teasing out a game
teasing out hands together.

Judgements not behind doors,
fair or unfair or good or bad,
a verdict is there
open to sky, field, pavilion.

In the shades of global faces
players come onto the scene.
Eyes and hands go crazy
after a run-about ball.

All of an art in it
with money-making in it
movements in body balance act
consume to consummation
to wild applause and shock
and silence and heartache.

And in popular strike of ball,
in crafted flight of ball,
new professors arrive, graduated
in seeing all sides *clear clear*

while entranced in the dance
with that wood and leather,
wooing that drive that tells
a game is never truly lost or won

A game played is
a field with scattered sounds
of musical instruments
taking part in a fusion.

# Haiku Moments: 1

**1**

Stems and leaves downy,
hidden here white under stone,
to be green sunlight.

**2**

Ouch! tongue! lime juice knifed,
needled, scalded, bitten with
this charged sunlight sting!

**3**

Still *hot hot* fanning –
wish I stood barefeet in one
big field of new snow!

**4**

Mango – you sucked from
sunrise to sunset to be
this ripe scented flesh.

**5**

Settled in the bowl
alone, banana lies there
cuddled-curved, waiting.

# Ritual Sun Dance

O sun O sun,
noon eye of noon time breath
makes blooms come,
unfolds big trees from seeds,
stirs crusts into leaves,
dresses cold shapes *warm warm*,
excites the little grown
to be fully grown.
        Hey-hey! Hey-hey!
        Sun gone down. Gone down underground.
        Come dance, come dance!
        Don't mind who father is.
        Don't mind who father is.
        Come dance and see the sun come back!

O sun O sun –
kisser who tickles crusts,
who swells yams in the ground,
fattens up droopy reeds
like apples and plums
like bananas and mangoes,
like sharp spices sharper –
touch everywhere.

Hey-hey! Hey-hey!
Sun gone down. Gone down underground.
Come dance, come dance!
Don't mind no child, no herd.
Don't mind your sound of words.
Come dance and see the sun come back!

O sun O sun –
flood-flame of air,
making pods pop
making seeds drop,
grass growing to strong rum,
oranges getting brighter,
grapes getting sweeter –
drape fields, drape fields.
Hey-hey! Hey-hey!
Sun gone down. Gone down underground.
Come dance, come dance!
Don't mind what roof house is.
Don't mind what kind dress is.
Come dance and see the sun come back!

O sun O sun –
mighty dazzler
who moves on the zero hour,
makes nuts brown,
brushless,
noiseless.

Only One of Me

Hey-hey! Hey-hey!
Sun gone down. Gone down underground.
Come dance, come dance!
Don't mind what track leads you.
Don't mind what wheels bring you.
Come dance and see the sun come back!

# Thatch Palms

Small settlement of Thatch Palms,
here beside the sea,
I come to see you.

Living in turbulent face of the sea,
umbrella leaves shadow clifftop.
Trunks all straight and smooth,
roots grip rocks like ironclaws.

An old tree is a standing pole,
bare of limbs,
time and wind beheaded.

I pick up
a dropped broad leaf:
so well ribbed
it flies from my hand
like a kite
into the sea.

I hug
a living tree.
I wonder at
the straightness
of Royal Palms
and at
the plumed show
of Queen Palms
and at
the timeless crops
of Date Palms.

I remember
monkey face
of fallen coconuts
will burst
into growth
after months
at sea, drifting.

And people go
from here
and knit palms
into roofs
and brooms
into hats
and mats
into baskets
and novelties.

I wonder at
the guardian
stance of palms.
I wonder at
their beginning.

I wonder at
the stubborn nature
of the fanlike leaves.

# Look, No Hands

Without muscles, without an arm or hand grip,
look how I wind bend back trees' big limbs.

Without wheels, without a down-hill,
look how I the sea roll and roll along.

Without a hurt, without a bruise,
look how I waterfall tumble down rocks.

Without bricks, without hammer or nails,
look how I tree build a house for birds.

Without apprenticeship, without DIY store,
look how I eagle build my family's nest.

Without getting even one single penny,
look how we apple trees give up our red apples.

Without a hose, without a sprinkler,
look how I sky water gardens with my rain.

# Rain Friend

All alone out-a deep darkness
two mile from Aunt Daphne
little Dearie – knee high little Dearie –
come push door open,
sodden with rain to hair root
all through to thin black skin
from naked foot bottom.

And she stand up there giggling.
A-say she did like the sea
the sky throw pon her,
coming down all over her
like say all her friends in it too
running about pasture and dark trees.

And when she did close her eyes and laugh
she hear Cousin Joe jackass braying
and Great House dog them barking
and road-water carry and carry her
like she a sailing boat in darkness.

# Goodmornin Brother Rasta

Good-days wash you mi brother
a-make peace possess you
and love enlightn you
a-make you givin be good
and you everymore be everybody
a-make Allness affect you always
and you meetn of eye to eye be vision
and all you word them be word of wonderment

# Watching a Dancer

She wears a red costume for her dance.
Her body is trim
and shapely and strong.

Before she begins
she waits composed,
waiting to hear the music start.

The music moves her.
She hears it keenly. The music
pulses her body with its rhythms.

It delights her. It haunts her body
into patterns of curves and angles.
She rocks. She spins.

She stretches entranced. She looks
she could swim and could fly.
She would stay airborne from a leap.

Her busy head, arms, legs, all know
she shows how the music looks.
Posture changes and movements are

the language of the sounds, that
she and the music use together
and reveal their unfolding story.

# Village Man Hot News

Tonight – jumpup!
Jumpup tonight!
Dance!
Dance up at Johnmariddle house.
Johnmariddle win thousn pound.
Johnmariddle board and grass a-suffer tonight.
Warman nod-nod with he big guitar.
Tonman rumble bass-fiddle like drum.
Little Cita a-sing.
Rum. Ice. Jerk-pork. Patty.
Come dance to moon till mornin soon!

Tonight – jumpup!
Jumpup tonight!
Dance!
Dance up at Johnmariddle house.
Johnmariddle win thousn pound.
Capital-K beat drums like he a-beat racehorse.
Wailerman trumpet a-streak moonshine.
While-a-yard of moon a-shake up.
Sol-o honey sax groan.
Rum. Ice. Jerk-pork. Patty.
Come dance to moon till mornin soon!

*jerk-pork – barbecue pork*

# Nana Krishie the Midwife

So keen on me those old eyes
the tracked black face
flowed with light

The tongue and gum ladled
stubborn words remembering
how I the boy child had knocked
thirty years before and hustled her
to come to the little cottage

Come with owl's wisdom and red
calico bag of tricks
to end labour: snap
and smack a newborn to cry

And now she looked at me surprised
and not at all surprised I had
come back from abroad
looking in a widened range
out of miracles she used and knew
time had discredited

For her ancestor's knack –
her tabooed secrets – now worked
in books of others
as ancient practices

Dreaming in her illiterate life
I felt the faltering tones
her startling shivered voice
thanking God
for showing me ever so well

# Everywhere Faces Everywhere

Again fascination holds me
in a London innercity classroom.
Holds me in these shades of eyes
around me in faces
plum-blue to nutmeg-brown,
melon-gold to peach-pale,
from nearby districts here.

The young gather
with old symbols of
the Anvil and the Acorn
and the Golden Stool
and the Egg and Lotus
and the Crescent and Star
and the Pomegranate
and the Star of David
and the Yin and Yang.
Different knowings have worked their ways
towards different seasonings.

I am in wonder. My own days at school
returned always with only
our all-similar flock of faces.

I am centred on this togetherness
of children. Who ocean-crossed differently.
Who were a mystery of strange blooms.
Who were like missing parts of a circle
that simply arrived. And no official,
no ministry, no boardroom, planned it.

I look up – considering.
This old stone building here.
Its imperial coffer-share.
Is this how inheritors are made?

Is time showing me
a little movement
of human growing?
Through secret workings
of the left hand? While
the ever busy right hand
hammered, hammered, fixing?

*Anvil – Nordic symbol, meaning creation*
*Acorn – Nordic symbol, meaning long life*
*Golden Stool – Ashanti gold stool: symbol of unity*
*Egg and Lotus – Hindu symbol of health and eternity*
*Crescent and Star – Islamic religious symbol*
*Pomegranate – Semitic symbol meaning abundance*
*Star of David – symbol of Judaism*
*Yin and Yang – Chinese symbol of balance in the creation principle*

# Haiku Moments: 2

### 1

Fife-man fife-man O
yu flutin dance in mi head –
see, me walk with it.

### 2

Like the flame tree's blooms,
leaf plumes of banana trees
*wave wave* to blue sky.

### 3

Full church is in song
for Jesus, born on this date:
holy – this arrest!

# Trap of a Clash

Noise of two dogs alarms like ten.
A terrible tussle and tangle here.
A swopping of bites and yelps
as dogs brace each other, up on back legs.
They fall, busy with attack –
all in a panic –
with tossing heads vicious
with quick yap-yaps for bone crush
with bared ripper teeth snarl fixed
with a grab for a grab
with jaw-grip for jaw-grip through flesh.
Each one in a trap, in a struggle.
Neither can let the other go.
Hurt, cries, terror, hold them
till now. Torn and punctured enough
they split. One goes
off home with a limp,
the other with a sorrowful whimper.

# Child-body Starving Story

Head misshapen and patchy with hair
  with shocked eyes in a hole with a stare

cheeks collapsed in skin among bones
  with cracked lips having not one moan

ears keeping a nonstop whining sound
  with neck hardly more than a broom-handle hold

hunched up shoulders v-shaped
  with twiggy arms claws-fingered

a belly all self pumped-up
  and knees the knotted marbles thinly skin wrapped

legs the drumsticks knee-knockers
  with feet not finding a body to carry together –

show me off, as this body-exhibit labelled,
'A NOT-ENOUGH-TO-SHARE LEFT-OUT'
and other times labelled,
'A GOVERNMENT'S NON-CARING LEFT-OUT'.

# Granny Begs Daughter Janie

Janie! Janie. Don't!
Please. *Don't* beat Boysie!
Pile in no more knocks.
More rocks on him, this is.
Do. Please. Don't.
Badness well schooled him.
It's others you beat through him.
Our boy. With all-time hurt.
Our boy. With shirt patchy-patchy.
    Stop the beating!
    Janie. Janie. Stop it!

Dear Janie. Miss Janie.
Please. *Don't* beat Boysie!
Remember. He's short of a dad.
Short and short. No father.
Lacks reared him. He swelled and swelled
for overdoses of good.
Not force. Not force and battering.
    Stop the beating!
    Janie. Janie. Stop it!

Dear Janie. Miss Janie.
Enough. Enough!
Don't drive him in with crooks.
We'll try coaxing him with books.
No more pain in this young frame.
Give more coaxing. No more hitting.
No more getting him knotted.
We want him heartened. Heartened.
Yes. Yes. Give me Boysie
Boysie? Our one-day big man Boysie?

# Okay, Brown Girl, Okay

*for Josie, nine years old, who wrote to me saying,*
*'Boys called me names because of my colour. I felt very upset*
*. . . my brother and sister are English. I wish I was, then I*
*won't be picked on . . . How do you like being brown?'*

Josie, Josie, I am okay
being brown. I remember,
every day dusk and dawn get born
from the loving of night and light
who work together, like married.
       And they would like to say to you:
       Be at school on and on, brown Josie
       like thousands and thousands and thousands
       of children, who are brown and white
       and black and pale-lemon colour.
       All the time, brown girl Josie is okay.

Josie, Josie, I am okay
being brown. I remember,
every minute sun in the sky
and ground of the earth work together
like married.
       And they would like to say to you:
       Ride on up a going escalator
       like thousands and thousands and thousands
       of people, who are brown and white
       and black and pale-lemon colour.
       All the time, brown girl Josie is okay.

Josie, Josie, I am okay
being brown. I remember,
all the time bright-sky and brown-earth
work together, like married
making forests and food and flowers and rain.
And they would like to say to you:
Grow and grow brightly, brown girl.
Write and read and play and work.
Ride bus or train or boat or aeroplane
like thousands and thousands and thousands
of children, who are brown and white
and black and pale-lemon colour.
All the time, brown girl Josie is okay.

# Other Side of Town

Talking faces
Wear the blues
Of singing faces

Thoughtful faces
Wear the blues
Of vocal faces

Laughing faces
Wear the blues
Of sad faces

Hopeful faces
Wear the blues
Of hopeless faces

Dressed up faces
Wear the blues
Of poverty faces

Sober faces
Wear the blues
Of drunken faces

Praying faces
Wear the blues
Of swearing faces

Love swoon faces
Wear the blues
of hatestruck faces

Clean free faces
Wear the blues
Of jail faces

O other side of town
Your sad faces
Are blues faces

# Innercity Youth Walks and Talks

He walks along with me and talks.
Says, 'Yes. I'm a fulltime
graffiti artist, and busy
with a real job what I like.'

Says, 'My style's my own style.
All artists know my work
and could get my message
on wall, in train, in bus,
on chimney, lamppost,
drainpipe, pavement, wherever.'

He says, 'I baffle heads of the town
with strategic secret signs.
Gives me a real buzz that.
Indoors sitting down.
How my art strikes people
just for the look at it.

'Satisfaction work that.
Takes art to the public.
Makes you vegetarian.

'For a lift inside and a cool
my dad settled on 'the weed'.
For a lift inside and a cool
I look for fresh work ideas.
To hide from faces
my dad lives in dark glasses.
To hide from faces, I look up
my night-time secret work.

'Yes,' he says. 'Risk of the job is
the risk of any job.
A work with height and depth
keeps eyes open round the head
for rail repairmen coming
or light of train dashing up
and keeps you nippy as a rat.'

Says, 'My mom took to a wig
to look like Tina Turner.
Mister Big my brother swears
nobody likes him
and he's stuck with that.
My dad doesn't get a pay,
doesn't get praises,
respect or adventure.
I make art in danger places.
And it's a buzz travelling daytime
seeing my secret signs everywhere.'

Says, 'Everybody has a downside
My downside takes to height.
Nobody in my family took to art.
Why not go for it I said.'

Says, 'Managed big gold buckle belt
with head of African king on it.
But I want a Suzuki bike
and can't manage it.
So I go for getting grimed
in city rubbish in corners.
Getting stuck between walls.
But it's a satisfaction work.'

# Song of White-People Ghosts

Why don't you come with me –
come on with me and see
red face duppies in a picnic feast
under cotton tree –
under cotton tree!
in a middleday sun-hot?

Why don't you come with me –
come on and hear and see
pretty talk in a tittle-tattle
to fork-plate-and-spoon tinkle-tinkle
under cotton tree,
in a middleday sun-hot?

Why don't you come with me –
come on with me and see
ladies taking pin eat peas
all dainty-dainty if you please
under cotton tree!
in a middleday sun-hot?

# Trick a Duppy

If you wahn trick a duppy
and wahn walk on *happy happy*
in a moonshine – bright moonshine –
hear how and how things work out fine.

You see duppy. No whisper. No shout.
Make not the least sound from you mouth.
One after the other *straight straight*,
strike three matchsticks alight.
Drop one then two of the sticks ablaze
and before you walk a steady pace
flash dead last match like you drop it
when *smart smart* it slipped in you pocket
to have duppy haunted in a spell
and why so you cannot tell.

But duppy *search search* for third matchstick
to vanish only when 6 a.m. come tick.

*Duppy – a ghost*

# Haiku Moments: 3

1
Here along roadside
yellow of gorse announces
sunlight is coming!

2
Stopped here listening –
this heedless grind of traffic
staggers the birdsongs.

3
To benches, to grass,
offices fall out for lunch –
sunlight's on London!

# Love is Like Vessel

Love is like vessel
that is mother and is father
and is nature parts
that become pure water.

Love is like face of ground
kissing feet
under whatever
bodyweight it greets.

It is like elements
that together make night
and elements
that together make light.

It is like carrying
a head that makes no weight
and also like quiet warmth
around cold hate.

Love is like finished work
with mixes so well wed
that grain, milk, yeast, heat are balanced
offering a *fine fine* bread.

Love is like roundness
of a running wheel
over a bumpy road
or one simply smooth like steel.

# A Nest Full of Stars

# Not One Weak Day

Monday comes –
it is that mighty shock
of a mind-jogging day.

Tuesday comes –
it is that tuning-in and getting-on
of a no-choosing day.

Wednesday comes –
it is that walled-in work
of a middle-week day.

Thursday comes –
it is that tough exploration-trip
of a tumbling-over-bumpy-waves day.

Friday comes –
it is that fattening feast
of a frying-up and fast-food day.

Saturday comes –
it is that shop, swim, play
of a swish-about day.

Sunday comes –
it is that special sparkler
of a little Christmas Day.

# Sometimes

Sometimes
I help with getting supper
Other times
I help with the grass-cutter.

Sometimes
I help with classroom clear-ups.
Other times
I'm not blameless over a trip-up.

Sometimes
I act soft and woolly.
Other times
I stand up to a bully.

Sometimes
I am hairy, tough, scary.
Other times
I am just a well-washed and brushed
sweet-smelly, cutey baby.

# Big Page Writer

Just carrying on writing
like a hard-working explorer
I suddenly have a full half page
making me a real big page writer.

Voices of alphabet-shapes, welcome
like eyeballs, birds' footprints, twigs, pebbles
from my head down through my pen
to be talking squiggles.

Flat out, writing, exploring I get
marked: CAN DO BETTER, or just, GOOD:
when, all silent – full of great voices –
my big half page holds a mighty *magic* mood.

# Sly Force Waiting

I knew that horrible
hunger-strength of my jaws
when I last bit my tongue.

I knew that dreadful
ducking-hold of water
when I fell into a swimming pool.

I knew that swallowing
slide of a pit, when I dropped
into a beach sand-hole.

# The Adding Up of Birthdays

People say:
You shove in your food like a spade
yet can't even slice bread straight.

You gawp at others' heaped plate
yet broke your nose just trying to skate.

You can't even get yourself up, awake
without even having stayed up late.

You are always the one with mucked-up hair
at home, at school, everywhere.

You are the only one to walk and not run
and, that one, with shoelaces flapping, undone.

I say:
I have my great hope in that special day
which every year adds on *another* BIRTHDAY!

# Somewhere! Somewhere!

Take me somewhere –
to the circus:
to spinning wheels and noisy bells.
Blazing stripes and streaks of yells.
Seeing swingers and clowns
round and round ceilings and walls.

Take me somewhere –
to the fair:
make me dither, jump, slither.
Make me slide and glide on feet and side.
Let me leap through hoops
and feel I move with pounding hooves.

Take me somewhere –
to a big street carnival:
finding drummers and bright dancers.
Getting my mouth all fishy, meaty,
peppery, spicy, buttery, sugary
while music and revelry make me giddy.

Take me somewhere –
to wide open countryside.
Let me redden and blacken
my tongue with berries and cherries.
Let me skip and flip in a trip.
Take me somewhere.

# Fireworks

Bang after bang tosses out
star and sunlit pieces
in a lit-up shower, drifting down.

In a slow party dance
meshed in bright shapes
of glowing lacework, like

necklaces, branches, arrows,
all drift down in
flame-pieces, rain-sparkled.

A fantastic Christmas tree of space
disappears before your eyes –
making you know the saddest goodbye.

# At the Showing-off Event

Centipedes all say: Watch numberless
needle legs together, walking.

Snakes all say: Watch how piles
of coiled ropes come alive!

Dogs all say: Even a playful bark is
terror to thieves hiding. Dogs, come on,
for one minute, *let's bark something crazy!*

Mother birds tell baby birds: No!
No parading for you.
You need weeks to get dressed.

Wind says: Trees, let's work up
*hard* windy weather – now!

# People Equal

Some people shoot up tall.
Some hardly leave the ground at all.
        Yet – people equal. Equal.

One voice is a sweet mango.
Another is a non-sugar tomato.
        Yet – people equal. Equal.

Some people rush to the front.
Others hang back, feeling they can't.
        Yet – people equal. Equal.

Hammer some people, you meet a wall
Blow hard on others they fall.
        Yet – people equal. Equal.

One person will aim at a star.
For another, a hilltop is *too far*.
        Yet – people equal. Equal.

Some people get on with their show.
Others never get on the go.
        Yet – people equal. Equal.

# Wild Whistling Woman

Wild whistling woman whistles up
    windy weather

Windy weather whistles up
    wrecking water working.

Wrecking water working whistles up
    wettest workless Wednesday.

Wettest workless Wednesday whistles up
    wild waterways of welcome water.

# Skeleton Sisters

Seven skeleton sisters all slowly
swallowed seven small, scrappy suppers.
And, Sunday-fed, soothed and satisfied,
each sister sang and sang her sweetest,
till sisters all sighed softly
and seemed ever so slightly swelled.

# Gobble-Gobble Rap

Me do a whispa and a big shout
with a meat-and-a-sweet mouth
like a non-meat, non-fish, puddn mouth
which is – a sleeper-waker, want-it-want-it mouth
which is – a take it, break it, eater mouth
which is – a gobble-gobble mouth

Me do a whispa and a big shout
with an oily-oily, salty-pepper mouth
like any seafood, wing-food, ground-food mouth
which is – a want-more-now, want-more-now mouth
which is – a chopper-chopper, swallow-down mouth
which is – a gobble-gobble mouth

Me do a whispa and a big shout
with a bony-and-a-fleshy meaty mouth
like a buttered-up, creamed up, oiled-up mouth
which is – a smile-and-smile, fries-and-fish mouth
which is a loud, bossy-bossy mouth
which is – a gobble-gobble mouth

Me do a whispa and a big shout
with a bun-and-cake and ice cream mouth
like a shopping for a cupboard mouth
which is – a mouthy, eat-eat, noisy mouth
which is – a break-it-up, bite-it-up mouth
which is – a gobble-gobble mouth.

Me do a whispa and a big shout
with a pie, chocolate and apple mouth
like any chatty-chatty, suck-sweet mouth
which is – a on-and-off, laugh-and-laugh mouth
which is – a gimme-gimme-more mouth
which is – a gobble-gobble mouth.

Me do a whispa and a big shout
with always that ready mouth about
like even that slurper-burper mouth
which is – a raver-craver, seeker mouth
which is – a singer and kissy-kissy mouth
which is – a gobble-gobble mouth
        which is – a gobble-gobble mouth.

# The Quarrel

Jan and Gemma quarrelled.
Gemma spoke about Jan's dog
as 'only a mongrel'.

Jan said, 'If not really
nasty, that was unkind.'

Gemma said, '*Mongrel* is
neither nasty nor unkind.'

'Yes,' Jan insisted:
'mongrel is not a kind word.
Especially when
"only" is attached to it.'

'Perhaps,' Gemma said. 'But
not *terrible, terrible,* is it?'

Jan said: 'Call my dog
"A mixed breed", that is fine.
But – not "*only a mongrel*".'

Gemma said: 'All right, Jan.
Suppose – I give you a fudge.'

Jan said: 'That would be friendly.
Especially – if "sorry"
is written on it, in ink.
And you give me another
one, to give back to you.
With "sorry" on it in ink.'

'Splendid,' Gemma said. 'Splendid.'
Silent, for a little while,
both girls ate a fudge, carefully.

# Together

I love it when we play
cricket or football
or sit and watch a game on TV.

Best of all
I love it when we swing together
and never stop
talking and laughing together
while we meet, all
passing each other on two swings
fitted to the same frame.

Then we go and buy
and eat ice cream slowly.
Yet, best of all
I love it when we swing together
talking and laughing, all
when passing each other.

# Singing with Recordings

We lick same stick of ice cream.
We tickle each other to screams.

Just as each catches the ball from each
we leap the other's back with a touch.

Knowing each one's hating and loving
we rush with whispers to our hiding.

We get buried in sand together.
We sing with recordings together.

We blow that one lucky-dip whistle.
We share our once used tissue.

Like two head-to-tail horses
there, standing in the rain
we get showered together again and again.

# Ball Gone Dialogue for Five

'Go and get the ball,'
>                (Nick shouts.)

'It's gone over the wall,'
>                (Ken says.)

'Sure, it's gone over the wall!'
>                (Nate says.)

'That Rottweiler is there,'
>                (Ken says.)

'Go on. Forget your fear,'
>                (Nick says.)

'I'll put the ladder down,'
>                (Kate says.)

'Yes, Put the ladder down,'
>                (Elton says.)

'My leg'll get hacked,'
>                (Ken says.)

'Tell leg: drag the dog back,'
>                (Nate says.)

'Go and get the ball!'
>                (Nick shouts.)

'You go and get the ball!'
>                (Kate insists.)

'Don't you dare climb my wall!'
>                (Mr Eflock says.)

'Here. I'm throwing *back* your ball.'

# Right Mix Like Water

Dad says, like $H_2O$, you
only need right input in
right order, to have success
in anything you do.

I watched Dad and Mum
to see exactly how,
each time, they drove our car.

Nobody looking, I started
up the car and drove it
straight out of the garage.

Hard as I tried, I
could not reverse the car
back into the garage.

I switched it off.
I tiptoed upstairs
I played my music loudest.

Then I saw Mum thought
Dad moved the car. I wished
and wished Dad thought
Mum had moved it.

# Eyes on the Time

When I travel in a train
and I want other passengers
to look at their watches

I get my mum and dad
to mumble something to themselves
a little loudly, then look
at their watches with purpose.

Then I just sit back pop-eyed
counting how many people
do look at their watches.

# Going Away Haiku

Boots and bikes roof-racked –

only stop, ice cream – aren't we

off on holiday!

# Postcard Poem: Solo

Mum, you needn't have worried one bit.
I travelled fine, fine, solo. Carried
in steelbird-belly of music shows.
I ate two passengers' pudding twice.
Nibbled nothings nutty and chocolately.
Sipped cool Cokes. Had more nibbles.
All over mountain after mountain.
Over different oceans. Over
weird clouds, like snow hills
with trails of straggly shapes
drifting, searching. And strangers
talked – Germans going on big-fish hunt,
Italians to ride glass-bottomed boat,
a Dane to do snorkelling. Then, Mum,
I hopped from steelbird-belly, down among
sun-roasted people of a palmtree place.
Welcome to Jamaica, voices called out.
While family hugged a sweating me
and took me off. Other exotics
got collected up in cars and coaches
to be naked on beaches, while
steelbird stood there shiny-ready
for more come-and-go trips.

# Earthworm and Fish

Like a gown, it wears the ground
and in there it is found.
Outside, it wiggles and squirms.
       It is a naked earthworm.

Like a gown, it wears water
and shares that living-quarters.
Outside, soon, fish is dead.
       Is open air like heaven to a fish?

# Seashell

Shell at my ear –
come share how I hear
busy old sea in whispers.

Moans rise from ancient depths
in ocean sighs
like crowds of ghost monsters.

Waves lash and fall –
in roars and squalls
with all a mystery ahhh!

# Trapped

I only tried to set the trap
and didn't expect it to snap.
Feeling such a sudden whack
I endured such a lonely shock.
      I only tried to set the trap
      and didn't expect it to snap.

Flash of trap – with its spiked catcher –
fastened down my every finger.
Oh, how I cried and softly cried!
Getting so hurt, I could've died.
      I only tried to set the trap
      catch that banana-eating rat:
      and didn't expect it to snap.

# Thinking Before I Sleep

It's good seeing how –
like jaws biting into food
and scissors cutting into paper –
legs move, one after the other.

It's good seeing how –
like leaves falling –
birds flutter down
with open wings to settle.

It's good seeing how –
like a road or a foot-track –
water makes it own way, over
and between hills and rocks,
to flow on, in its own river bed.

# Taking Action

I dream I am
high flying duck's eyes
over an ocean, washed
in fire-splash sunset.

I dream I am
two swimming shark's eyes
in search of swallowed
whole-fish dinner.

I dream we cross an open field
and face a lion in our track.
Making one group-body, oddly, we
come together, thrusting arms like horns
and flapping our clothes like fighting
wings, while we scream in waves
like ear-splitting sirens.
The lion turns and runs in terror.

I dream I am
colour pieces of feelings
in music-notes, jumping up
on the keys of a piano
playing it together.
I dream of a lot that puzzles me.

# A Nest Full of Stars

Only chance made me come and find
my hen, stepping from her hidden
nest, in our kitchen garden.

In her clever secret place, her tenth
egg, still warm, had just been dropped.

Not sure of what to do, I picked up
every egg, counting them, then put them
down again. *All were mine.*

All swept me away and back.
I blinked, I saw: a whole hand
of ripe bananas, nesting.

I blinked, I saw: a basketful
of ripe oranges, nesting.

I blinked, I saw: a trayful
of ripe naseberries, nesting.

I blinked, I saw: an open bagful
of ripe mangoes, nesting.

I blinked, I saw:
a mighty nest full of stars.

# Caribbean Playground Song

Say, Good mornin, Granny Maama
Good mornin, Granpa Taata.
      Good mornin when it rainin.
      Good mornin when sun shinin.
         Good mornin.

Say, Good mornin, Miss Pretty-Pretty.
Good mornin, one-yeye Mista Shorty.
      Good mornin when sun shinin.
      Good mornin when hurrikaanin
         Good mornin.

Say, Good mornin, Mista Big-N-Fat-Man.
Good mornin, Mista Maaga Man.
      Good mornin when sun shinin.
      Good mornin when hurrikaanin
         Good mornin.

Say, Good mornin, Mista Lamefoot
Good mornin, dear Miss No-Toot.
      Good mornin when sun shinin.
      Good mornin when hurrikaanin
         Good mornin.

Say, Good mornin, dear-dear Bush Miss.
Good mornin, dear Mista Touris.
  Good mornin when sun shinin.
  Good mornin when hurrikaanin
    Good mornin.

Say, Good mornin, Granny Maama
Good mornin, Granpa Taata.
  Good mornin.


*one-yeye – one-eyed*
*Maaga – meagre or thin*
*No-Toot – No-tooth*
*Touris – tourist*

# Smooth Skippin

Skip a-show groun is evva too hot.
Easy. Easy. Whether thin or fat
a-listn poor man rattle quatty
as him go on all chatty-chatty.

Skip betta than doin a frog jump.
Skip betta than droppin on yu rump –
a-listn ol lady at fireside
a-tell bout the prettiest bride.
a-tell bout the prettiest bride.
a-tell bout the prettiest bride . . .

*a-show – showing*
*a-listn – listening*
*quatty – old sterling coins*
*a-tell – telling*

# Old Man Called 'Arawak'

Cos he coughed, coughed and choked
as he smoked, smoked and smoked
spitter man old Daddy Brock
got named Smoker Arawak.
      Got named Smoker Arawak.


Cos he ate only best bammy
made by best-loved granny
old man Mister Mack
got named Cassava Arawak
      Got named Cassava Arawak.


*bammy – a flat Jamaican cassava bread*

# He Loved Overripe Fruits

Hot sweaty body carrying treats
my Caribbean Grandpa came home
turned his pockets inside-out
and gave us runny, soft, sticky sweets.

Other times, the sweaty wet pockets
brought us bruised, overripe fruits
like bananas or blackberries

or, sometimes, mangoes, plums
gineps, naseberries
or a tempting mixture of these.

Other times we knew how
to push, tussle, compete hard
to take off Grandpa's boots.

Not always, but, often,
turned upside-down, the boots
carried small-change in them:
tipped out all round the floor,
as he smiled, seeing who got how much.

*ginep – big-tree fruit, bunched like grapes: creamy flesh
  covers its stones.*
*naseberry – sapodilla-plum: having sweet brown flesh.*

# Queen and King Mullets

King says, Queen Mullet, mam
yu so prettily pinky white
Oh, I love yu lovely sight.
      Oh, I love yu lovely sight.


Queen says, King Mullet, sar
yu beard is right.
Oh, yu beard is jus, jus, right.
      Oh, yu beard is just, jus, right . . .


*Mullet – goatfish variety with pair of long barbels*
  *below the mouth like a beard.*

# Doubtful Sayings

Take hot bad licks and nevva evva cry
you'll give some back before yu die.

Eat a big bug and dohn cough it up
jaws'll crack big nut with yu mouth shut.

Duppy eyes livin in a cut bamboo
will come to live in ragged ol shoe.

Dress in notn pretty and eat notn sweet
duppy'll hol you han as yu walk on street.

Eat yu food up fram pearl dishes
yu'll ketch fish beyond all wishes.
       You'll ketch fish beyond all wishes . . .

*licks – blows*
*ketch – catch*

# Duppy Dance

You walk too-too late at night
duppies make your wrong road the right.
Around you, they rattle strings of bones.
      And duppies dance. Duppies dance.

All along deep-deep dark road
duppies croak like huge hidden toad.
You hear distant scary bells toll.
      And duppies dance. Duppies dance.

Duppies make horses' hooves clop-clop.
Make some strange big birds flutter up.
Make you feel your skin gone shrivelled.
      And duppies dance. Duppies dance.

Roaring, snorting, like ten bulls,
duppies rip off your clothes – one pull!
Skeletons prance all around you.
      And duppies dance. Duppies dance.

*duppy – a ghost*

# Getting Bigger Rap

Watch me getting bigger and bigger
stepping wider, walking taller.

Nothing easier in a tussle
but now I'm better when I whistle

Barring too, that only game called 'dart'
I know much of who is who in sport.

And though no worm with book-intake look
I sometimes do know a latest book.

See me how my clothes are cut in style
all ready to walk down the aisle.

See how more and more I'm on the ball
and it's little bother if I fall.
   And it's little bother if I fall.

   Watch me getting bigger and bigger
       stepping wider, walking taller higher
             stepping wider, walking taller higher . . .

# Woods Whisperings

We woods whisper. We whisper:
You will find in us
whole naked families
of roofs, floors, beds, toothpicks,
chest-of-drawers, bats, walking-sticks.

We woods whisper. We whisper:
You will find in us
naked mask families
of gods, devils, clowns
and even faces of lions.

We woods whisper. We whisper:
You will find in us
whole naked families
of flutes, with one the bamboo,
one the deep-voiced didgeridoo.

We woods whisper. We whisper:
You will find in us
whole naked families
of carved girls and boys –
all faces of toys.

We woods whisper. We whisper:
You will find in us
whole naked families
of rocking horses.
We woods come and live in your houses.

# Granddad's Visitor

After a good, big supper
Granddad dozed off
in his comfy chair.

Granddad woke to see
he had a sitting visitor
looking at him with a strange smile.

Granddad knew the visitor.
He smiled, saying, 'Hello!'
Getting up he moved towards

his visitor, stretching for
a handshake. Then horror
wipped away Granddad's smile.

No one was sitting there.
Puzzled, Granddad shuffled
back to his chair and sat.

Looking up, he saw
the visitor was still there.
He knew the visitor.

He got up again to greet
his visitor. As he turned
round, he saw only the chair.

Granddad stood a while.
Then he sat down again.
When he looked up slowly
no one was there.

# Mister-ry

Wild New-Forest Pony takes my apple.
Eats my banana too. Looks for more.
I stroke him. He follows me. So strangely
friendly towards me, he makes me
suddenly name him, MISTER-RY. And, more.
Next morning – shocks me out of bed.

Arched back with long legs and neck
crops grass, in our front garden. I
rush out calling MISTER-RY! MISTER-RY!
In a low rumble of a neigh, he comes –
long face pushing, nuzzling me.

Our dog, WORRIER, dashes about,
teasing MISTER-RY to play with him.
Picking him up, I put WORRIER lying
flat on the back of the horse. All
on his own he walks with dog rider
round and round the garden. Then, my go.

Holding neck and mane, I climb up,
sit erect, having my trotting ride
round the garden, when, along my
street side, a blast of applause shakes me
and goes on through my barebacked ride,
never stopping. I say, OK, MISTER-RY.

Sharp, sharp, he stops. I dismount,
looking. I see THE QUEEN. Clapping too
THE QUEEN is there, saying to me,
Give him a drink now. Give him a drink.

I run into the house. Get a bucket
of water. Come back with it, panting
with new disbelief.

     No horse is there.
          No audience is there.
In the far, far distance I hear
wild clattering of hoofs going,
     going away . . .

# New Poems

# Top Footballer Rap

See quicker kicker in the grass arena:
my Mister Wizard taker and a passer.
His kickers and headers clock-up top scorer
to rave-rage of the colour sports page –
      to rave-rage of the colour sports page.

See quicker kicker in the grass arena:
meeting every ball as a challenge for a goal
and it's a rabbit running how he hounds it –
passion man of a play-ball occasion –
      passion man of a play-ball occasion.

See quicker kicker in the grass arena:
Mister Boot with foot with quick-quick shoot
getting loudest roar of the crowd
for footballer who is bliss –
      for footballer who is bliss.

See quicker kicker in the grass arena:
quickest taker. Swiftest passer and blocker.
Shooter and goal finder. Opposition frustrator.
Man of endless daring with foot looting.
Prince of the football patch, whose ball snatch
again and again wins the match –

    Mr Slappy-Slappy Happiness.

    Mr Slappy-Slappy –
        all happiness.

    Mr Slappy-Slappy –
        all happiness.

            All happiness.

# Looking at the Painting: 'Fin d'Arabesque' by Edgar Degas

She is that special expression of dance.
Other dancers are at ease off-stage.
She ends a programme and highlights it.

In performance with the company
her lines of movements all stood out
clean, in the music, rhythms.

Now concealing tiredness and aches
she performs end like beginning:
controlled, graceful, effortless.

Open-armed, she holds out her
bouquet, bowing to discipline applauded
for the triumph of dance.

And arms, legs, costume, encircling
her, she looks dreamlike, as if she blooms
under leaves-filtered moonlight.

# Love of Love

I love the love turned movement
love and love turned enjoyment

I love the love turned light and seeing
love and love turned night and knowing

I love the love turned mother
love the love turned father

I love the love turned summer
love the love turned water

I love the love turned fire
love the love turned desire

I love the love turned diaphanous air in a whirl
love the love turned girl

I love the love turned joy
love the love turned boy

I love the love turned taste of sun
love the love turned smell of rain

I love the love turned death and birth
love the love turned earth

I love the love turned comfort when alone
love the love turned stone

I love the love of love
and how I feel a song of love

# Longings

Longings come grabbing me lately
for a broad black belt,
the widest white hat,
pointed red shoes with
impossible high heels,
dazzing earrings, and silver
strings of spreading beads
brushing my waist.

Longings come itching me
to be much more leggy
sitting slimly crosslegged
having long fingernails.

I look in the mirror. God!
I am small featured and so flat!
I have dirty hands and fingernails.
My hair cries out
for total reconstruction-work.

Longings hit me
to change my weekends
to see myself
newly
and totally unrecognisable.

# Earth and Beyond

In shining silver suit streaked with gold,
tall and thin person stood beside me.
'Hello, Spacecrosser,' she said.
'I am Sva.'
'Hello,' I said, and saw I changed
into shining silver suit streaked
with gold, like her own and the sunny
sweep of white tent-like buildings.

'This is Village Svala,' Sva said, 'where
your heart had longed and longed to see.'
'Wonderful,' I said. 'Fantastic!'

Inside, a tent-like building was
open-topped and had windows, but
all its space was empty, except
for a fragrance of flowers.

'People work here,' Sva said. Instantly,
in white streaked with silver and gold,
people for work came in emptyhanded
and sat down meditation-style.

Piece by piece, musical instruments
began appearing, settling together
and started tuning themselves up.

Sva took me round, showed me things.
I loved best those sunrise-colour
waterboats, made only of sunrise
colour water. All floating, they
gave rides to children around hills.

I loved the heavenly bodies
in display – the stars and moon
with all the signs of the zodiac,
ending with great flashes
of darkness and fire.

Oh, my mum was coming to get me!
I must remember, how people
in Svala don't sleep, they only
meditate on it some minutes.
No roads – people arrive or go
about by only thinking it.
I rode inside a drifting moon,
looking out the window.

# Two Stories

## 1: Bush Accident Message

Mummah Mummah and Buddy and Sis
Dear-Dear break her leg

her *clean clean* young-girl leg
up at Highrock Pass

After she didn get far
her load go fall on her

O she drop down 'biff'
pop her leg like a stick

like a sometn a load-up donkey mash
and flesh and bone pop-up with the mash

Dear-Dear break her leg
Lord her *clean clean* young-girl leg

and they bringin her droopy
O bringin her droopy
on Mister Mack donkey

# 2: Town Dentist Haiku

Her hands like a child's
work her flute sonata voice
and pull out my tooth.

# Draped With Water

See how my diving dip
launches me down and up.

See me take to water
all a water stroker.

Pushing like a monster frog
I am no drift log.

Silver spread of water
drapes me from the collar.

With my water-dress on
it's a slow-motion run.

Here, each facedown movement
brings me fresh contentment.

Strangely, I feel I fly
taking depths under sky.

And, see, I am deeper:
well in with big water.

Then breaking the waves' backs
I ride on for the rocks.

Now, in a stone recess
I feel water-caress.

Like a seal glistening
I feel I flash lightning.

See me sitting tired:
see me happily stirred.

# Anancy John-Canoo Song

Poor Tatty-Tatty-Pappy.
Poor Pitchy-Patchy-Pappy –
Lost yesterday and he lost tomorrow.
He doesn't rent and he doesn't borrow.
He finds a fine-fine blackskin gal
And she finds a better-better pal.

O, they cuss him and cuss-cuss him.
They cuss him and they cuss him.
Whai-O, they cuss-cuss him!
Can't guess any riddle-mi-riddle
But what a John-Canoo-man, John-Canoo-man,
John-Canoo-man, John-Canoo-man, John-Canoo-man, O!
        Tatty-Tatty-Pappy.
                Pitchy-Patchy-Pappy.

Poor Tatty-Tatty-Pappy.
Poor Pitchy-Patchy-Pappy –
Lost yesterday and he lost tomorrow.
He doesn't rent and he doesn't borrow.
He finds a fine-fine fairskin gal
And she finds a better-better pal.

O, they cuss him and cuss-cuss him.
They cuss him and they cuss him.
Whai-O, they cuss-cuss him!
Can't guess any riddle-mi-riddle
But what a John-Canoo-man, John-Canoo-man,
John-Canoo-man, John-Canoo-man, John-Canoo-man, O!
     Tatty-Tatty-Pappy.
          Pitchy-Patchy-Pappy, O! . . .

(From the 'John-Canoo and the Shine-Dancer-Shine
Event' in *Anancy Spiderman* by James Berry.)

# Index of First Lines